W9-BCX-949

DATE DUE

980   BC#34880000074190 $30.00
SCO   Scoones, Simon
           South America

Morrill Elementary School
Chicago Public Schools
6011 South Rockwell Street
Chicago, IL 60629

CONTINENTS OF THE WORLD

SOUTH AMERICA

Simon Scoones

WORLD ALMANAC® LIBRARY

Please visit our web site at: www.worldalmanaclibrary.com
For a free color catalog describing World Almanac® Library's list of high-quality books and multimedia programs, call 1-800-848-2928 (USA) or 1-800-387-3178 (Canada). World Almanac® Library's fax: (414) 332-3567.

Library of Congress Cataloging-in-Publication Data

Scoones, Simon.
   South America / by Simon Scoones.
      p. cm. — (Continents of the world)
   Includes bibliographical references and index.
   ISBN 0-8368-5915-4 (lib. bdg.)
   ISBN 0-8368-5922-7 (softcover)
   1. South America—Juvenile literature. I. Title. II. Continents of the world (Milwaukee, Wis.)
F2208.5.S446   2005
980—dc22   2005043269

This North American edition first published in 2006 by
World Almanac® Library
330 West Olive Street, Suite 100
Milwaukee, WI 53212 USA

This U.S. edition copyright © 2006 by World Almanac® Library. Original edition copyright © 2005 by Hodder Wayland. First published in 2005 by Hodder Wayland, an imprint of Hodder Children's Books, a division of Hodder Headline Limited, 338 Euston Road, London NW1 3BH, U.K.

Commissioning editor: Victoria Brooker
Editor: Kelly Davis
Inside design: Jane Hawkins
Series concept and project management by
EASI-Educational Resourcing, (info@easi-er.co.uk)
Statistical research: Anna Bowden
World Almanac® Library editor: Barbara Kiely Miller
World Almanac® Library art direction: Tammy West
World Almanac® Library cover design: Dave Kowalski
World Almanac® Library production: Jessica Morris

Photo credits: Corbis cover, 12 (Bettmann), 18 (Reuters), 19 (Jhon Jairo Bonilla/Reuters), 24, 40, 45 (Ricardo Azoury), 39 (Julia Waterlow), 42 (Fulvio Roiter), 44 (Jeremy Horner), 46 (Paulo Whitaker), 47 (Enrique Marcarian), 51(t) (Antoine Serra/In Visu), 51(b) (David Mercado), 52 (Arianespace); EASI-Images 3, 8, 9(b), 14(both), 16, 21(b), 26, 27, 30, 34, 35, 57(both) (Simon Scoones), title page, 6, 23, 31, 36, 50 (Roy Maconachie); Mary Evans Picture Library 10, 11(both); Panos Pictures 33, 49, 59 (Jeremy Horner); Edward Parker 4, 9(t), 17, 28, 37, 38, 41, 48, 55, 58; Still Pictures 7 (Gerard and Margi Moss), 13, 25 (Russell Gordon), 20 (Kevin Schafer), 21(t) (Mike Kolloffel), 29, 32 (Mark Edwards), 43 (Janet Jarman), 53 (Ron Giling), 54 (Jeremy Woodhouse), 56 (C. Allan Morgan); Survival 22 (Fiona Watson). Maps and graphs: Martin Darlison, Encompass Graphics. Population Density Map © 2003 UT-Battelle, LLC.

Printed in China

1 2 3 4 5 6 7 8 9 09 08 07 06 05

At Iguazú (Iguaçu) Falls, which straddles the border between Brazil and Argentina, 259 waterfalls pour out about 6,500 cubic yards (5,000 cubic meters) of water every second.

CONTENTS

SOUTH AMERICA — A LAND OF EXTREMES

South America can boast of many record-breaking features. The continent has some of the world's biggest waterfalls, including the highest. The world's driest desert, Atacama, is found on the western side of the continent, while snaking across South America's lowlands is the mighty Amazon, a river that carries more water than any other on Earth.

South America rises to extremely high altitudes, too. In the west, life for people in Ecuador, Peru, and Bolivia is dominated by the Andes, the longest mountain chain on Earth, which stretches for over 5,000 miles (8,000 kilometers). Forced upward by the collision of vast interlocking pieces of rock that make up Earth's crust, known as plates, the highest peaks of the Andes rise steeply to nearly 23,000 feet (7,000 meters). The world's highest railway winds its way through the Andes in Peru, while in neighboring Bolivia, La Paz is the world's highest capital city.

Deforestation in the Amazon rain forest, Brazil.

In the north, Colombia, Venezuela, Guyana, Suriname, and French Guiana lie close to the equator. Much of this region is covered by dense tropical rain forest. Brazil has the biggest expanse of tropical rain forest in the world. Part of this vast natural environment is under threat from cattle ranchers, farmers, loggers, miners, and road builders. Everyone in the world will be affected by rain forest destruction. Plant species that could become new sources of food or medicine may be lost, and fewer trees will be left to soak up the carbon dioxide that contributes to global warming.

Further south, past the plains and cattle ranches of landlocked Paraguay, the republic of Uruguay, and northern Argentina, the climate cools until reaching Patagonia, a vast region of ice and snow. This freezing climate is shared by Argentina and Chile in the deep south, just a short hop from Antarctica.

Each South American country has its own character. Many enjoy relative wealth, thanks to the continent's plentiful supply of farmland, minerals, timber, and energy resources. South America has a population of about 370 million, and many people have moved to cities in search of a better quality of life. Here, industries produce goods for sale across the world. Yet the continent's riches are not equally shared, and it will be a massive challenge for governments to give all young South Americans a chance at a bright future.

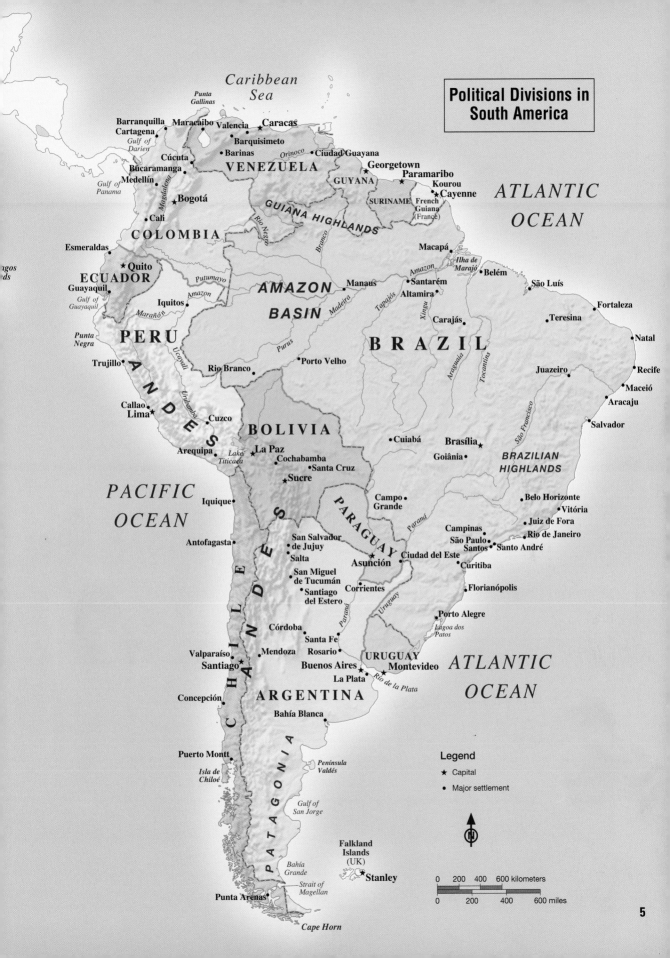

Political Divisions in
South America

Caribbean
Sea

Punta
Gallinas

Barranquilla
Cartagena Maracaibo Valencia Caracas
Gulf of   Barquisimeto
Darien   Cúcuta   Barinas   Ciudad Guayana
Bucaramanga   VENEZUELA   Georgetown
Gulf of   Medellín   Paramaribo
Panama   GUYANA   Kourou
              Bogotá   SURINAME Cayenne   ATLANTIC
                                                 French   OCEAN
              Cali   GUIANA HIGHLANDS   Guiana
                                                 (France)
COLOMBIA

Esmeraldas   Macapá
                                                 Ilha de
                     Putumayo   Santarém   Marajó
★ Quito   Belém
ECUADOR   AMAZON   Manaus   São Luís
Guayaquil   Amazon   Altamira
Gulf of   Iquitos   BASIN   Fortaleza
Guayaquil   Marañón   Carajás   Teresina
Punta   Natal
Negra   PERU   B R A Z I L
                     Purus   Porto Velho   Recife
Trujillo   Rio Branco   Maceió
                                                                 Aracaju
Callao   Ucayali   Salvador
Lima   Cuzco
Arequipa   BOLIVIA   Cuiabá   Brasília ★
            La Paz   Goiânia   BRAZILIAN
Lake   Cochabamba   HIGHLANDS
Titicaca   Santa Cruz
PACIFIC   ★ Sucre   Belo Horizonte
OCEAN   Vitória
Iquique   Campo   Juiz de Fora
                     Grande   Paraná   Campinas Rio de Janeiro
Antofagasta PARAGUAY   São Paulo Santos
San Salvador   Santos   Santo André
de Jujuy   Ciudad del Este Curitiba
Salta   Asunción ★
San Miguel   Corrientes   Florianópolis
de Tucumán
Santiago   Uruguay
del Estero   Porto Alegre
Córdoba   Paraná   Lagoa dos
Santa Fe   Patos
Valparaíso Mendoza Rosario   URUGUAY ATLANTIC
Santiago   Buenos Aires   Montevideo OCEAN
            La Plata   Río de la Plata
Concepción ARGENTINA

            Bahía Blanca

Puerto Montt
Isla de   Península
Chiloé   Valdés

            PATAGONIA   Gulf of
                        San Jorge

Bahía   Falkland
Grande   Islands
                     (UK)
Strait of   ★ Stanley
Magellan

Punta Arenas

Cape Horn

Legend
★ Capital
• Major settlement

0   200 400 600 kilometers

0   200 400 600 miles

5

1. THE HISTORY OF SOUTH AMERICA

DURING THE LAST ICE AGE, THE VERY FIRST PEOPLES IN THE Americas are thought to have crossed a temporary bridge of solid ice that linked Asia to the western coast of Alaska. Descendants of these people gradually spread southward in search of food. About eighteen-thousand years ago, some reached the plains, forests, and mountain ranges of present-day Colombia. These native groups of Indians, also called Amerindians by some, have lived in the rain forests of the Amazon basin for about fifteen-thousand years.

Further south, in Argentina, archaeologists discovered a cave covered in paintings of hands and hunting scenes hidden in the steep rock walls of a canyon, 164 feet (50 m) above the Rio Pinturas. The artists were the Tehuelche people who lived here beginning about 7000 B.C. and still live in Argentina today. They used the juice of local berries as paint, blown through the carved bone of a nandú, a South American relative of the ostrich. These ancient paintings have remained bright and colorful, thanks to the mixture of fats and urine used by the Tehuelche to preserve them.

For hundreds of years, llamas have been used for farming by the Aymara, Native people who live in Peru and Bolivia.

About the time of the Tehuelche's cave art, people began to adopt a more settled way of life. By crossbreeding wild plants, they created fields of domesticated potatoes, maize, beans, and peppers. They developed sophisticated irrigation techniques to water their fields and learned how to preserve food by freeze-drying it in the cold mountain air. They also tamed animals, such as dogs and llamas, to help with farm work.

● ● ● ● ● ● ➤ IN FOCUS: Nasca Lines

Flying over the stony desert in northern Peru in the 1930s, a scientist named Paul Kosok spotted vast drawings of animals, birds, and other patterns etched into the desert. In such a dry climate, rainwater had not washed away the drawings, which looked much as they had two thousand years earlier, at the time of the people of Nasca (a small town to the south). An early theory suggested that the patterns could be landing strips for aliens. Although this theory was dismissed long ago, no one is exactly sure why these images were drawn. Maria Reiche, a German mathematician, devoted her life to studying the Nasca lines. For more than fifty years, she charted the lines from both the air and a 50-foot- (15-m-) high platform. Reiche believed that the drawings mapped the position of the stars, providing an early form of calendar.

These Nasca lines, seen from the air, depict a gigantic spider. Researchers think that people began creating these images about 400 B.C. and continued to do so for another thousand years.

THE INCA EMPIRE

Farmers moved from Lake Titicaca and settled in the valleys around Cuzco, Peru. The great civilization of the Inca began here in about A.D. 1100. According to local legend, the first Inca ruler, Manco Capac, rose out of Lake Titicaca. After Manco Capac, a succession of Inca rulers, known as Sapa Inca, controlled Inca territory. Four viceroys looked after Sapa Inca's affairs in the four provinces of the empire. Below the viceroys, a governor had authority over ordinary people in each province.

The Inca were skilled architects and road builders. They built 14,000 miles (22,525 km) of roads, many of which can still be seen today. The Inca were expert farmers, too. Near Cuzco, they carved perfect amphitheaters of terraces and used them to learn what crops grew best at different altitudes. The Inca produced three thousand types of potato, maize (Indian corn), and other crops in these "open-air laboratories."

The Colca Canyon in southern Peru was a sacred place for the Inca. They believed it was the home of Nevado Ampato, a god who brought them good harvests. To please Nevado Ampato, the Inca led pilgrimages to the top of Mount Ampato,

In their great amphitheaters, the Inca could copy soil and moisture conditions at different elevations on the terraces. In this way, they could learn which crops would grow best in different places.

overlooking the canyon. Here, they would make the ultimate offering—the sacrifice of one of their own people. In 1995, the body of one of the sacrificial victims was found on the mountain and named Juanita. Thanks to the icy climate, Juanita's body and clothes were perfectly preserved, and they can tell us much about how the Inca lived.

Between A.D. 1100 and 1500, the Inca conquered other peoples and eventually commanded the biggest empire ever known in the Americas. They introduced the language of Quechua, which is still spoken by people in Bolivia, Colombia, Ecuador, and Peru.

This mummy is from the ancient Paracas culture, a group of people who lived in southwest Peru from 1300 B.C. to A.D. 200.

● ● ● ● ▶ IN FOCUS: The lost city of Machu Picchu

The ancient Inca city of Machu Picchu was discovered in 1911. Built on a ridge above the Urubamba River and at an altitude of 2,350 feet (7,710 m), Machu Picchu had been hidden in the jungle for hundreds of years. Although the forest has been cleared, mystery still surrounds these magnificent ruins.

Most people believe that noble Inca families and their servants lived in Machu Picchu, where they worshiped their sun god. But the fate of the city's residents remains unknown. Today, Machu Picchu is one of Peru's top tourist attractions.

More than three-hundred thousand people a year make the trek to visit Machu Picchu in Peru.

EUROPEAN INVADERS

At the height of their power in 1525, the Inca controlled an area bigger than the Roman empire, stretching about 2,485 miles (4,000 km) from northern Ecuador to southern Chile. The Inca empire was home to as many as twelve million people, one-third of all South Americans at the time. By the 1530s, however, the Inca empire had grown weak, and two sons of former ruler Huayna (or sometimes Wayna) Capac fought over who should succeed their father. At the same time, explorers from Europe had landed in different parts of the continent in search of gold and other precious metals. With only two hundred men, Spanish explorer Francisco Pizarro overcame the Inca empire in just two years. A great civilization that had lasted four hundred years was over, and much of the continent gradually fell under Spanish control. Many local people had to give up their land and were forced to work on plantations or to mine gold and diamonds.

A group of Incas is shown near a stone bridge that spans a waterfall, where they were first encountered by Francisco Pizarro and his men in about 1530.

Because the Spanish colonies were only permitted to trade with their colonial masters, all these natural riches were sent to Europe.

Other South American regions were also controlled by European powers. Brazil became a Portuguese colony, and French Guiana is still under French control today. Guyana and Suriname were British colonies. In about 1650, the British set up sugar and tobacco plantations on the banks of the Suriname

River. Two decades later, the Dutch took over after agreeing with the British to swap Suriname with New Amsterdam, or present-day New York.

DISEASE AND SLAVERY

The arrival of Europeans was disastrous for the Native people. In the early days, contact between Europeans and Natives was quite friendly, because the Europeans were fascinated by Native culture. Attitudes, however, soon changed. The invaders wanted to make the most of their conquered lands, and many Native people were murdered or forced to become plantation workers. Others died from diseases introduced by the Europeans, such as measles and smallpox, and many moved deeper into the Amazon rain forest. By the seventeenth century, so few Native people were left on the coast that slaves were shipped over from West Africa to work on the plantations.

In this artwork, West African slaves are shown being handed over to their Dutch master just after their arrival in Suriname in 1806.

Explorer and navigator Ferdinand Magellan discovered Chile's Strait of Magellan on a trip for Spain in November 1520.

FACT FILE

In the far south, European explorers encountered the Tehuelche people. Ferdinand Magellan, the first to meet them in 1520, claimed the Tehuelche were built like giants. He called them *pata gones* (meaning "large feet"). The Tehuelche territory in southern Argentina and Chile is now called Patagonia.

By the early 1800s, the Spanish had fallen behind both France and Great Britain as a world power. In 1808, French emperor Napoleon invaded Spain. News of Spain's troubles gave hope to those fighting for freedom in South America. Wars of independence broke out, and some parts of the continent changed hands once again.

HERO OF HEROES

Venezuelan-born Simon Bolívar became the hero of the independence movement. In Peru, the stronghold of the Spanish, Bolívar combined forces with General José de San Martín who had defeated Spanish forces in Argentina. Bolívar drove out the Spanish in Venezuela, Colombia, and Ecuador and won independence for Peruvians in 1821.

The territory southeast of Peru was renamed Bolivia in honor of General Simon Bolívar (1783–1830), shown in this painting.

FROM INDEPENDENCE TO DICTATORSHIP

Apart from French Guiana, the rest of South America gained independence during the 1800s. In many countries, however, power was kept in the hands of a few. In 1973, for example, General Augusto Pinochet Ugarte and his troops organized a coup to remove Salvador Allende, Chile's first freely elected president, who came to power in 1970. In the violence that followed the 1973 coup, Allende was killed, and Pinochet began a period of brutal dictatorship that lasted more than fifteen years.

In 1954, Alfredo Stroessner seized power in Paraguay and ruled for nearly thirty-five years. After World War II,

FACT FILE

In the early 1800s, Uruguay was a Spanish colony before being seized by Great Britain in 1807. Control was rewon by Spain, but it soon shifted to Argentina, then Portugal, and then Brazil. Uruguay finally gained its independence in 1825.

• • • • • ▶ IN FOCUS: Evita

In 1945, a beautiful actress named Eva Perón was adored across Argentina. Best known by the name Evita, Eva Perón was President Juan Perón's wife, and she made passionate speeches about the terrible living conditions of the poor. Using her influence on her husband, she forced a change in the law that allowed women to vote for the first time. When Evita died in 1952, the whole country went into mourning.

Paraguay became a haven for German Nazis escaping punishment for war crimes in Europe. Military dictatorships controlled Brazil and Argentina, too. In 1976, Argentina's military government began a "dirty war" to wipe out any opposition to its power. Up to thirty thousand people were tortured or secretly killed. The military government was humiliated, however, after President Leopoldo Galtieri's failed attempt to take the neighboring Falkland Islands from the British in 1982. The next year, the generals gave up power, and the Argentinian people were allowed to vote freely for their government. Today, people in South America can choose their leaders in free elections, but older generations have not forgotten the difficult years of living under a dictatorship.

On Thursdays, a group called the "Mothers of the Disappeared" still gathers in Buenos Aires to remember their loved ones who were victims of Argentina's "dirty war."

2. SOUTH AMERICAN ENVIRONMENTS

STRETCHING FROM THE EQUATOR SOUTH TOWARD ICY Antarctica, South America covers a great range of latitudes. The relief of the land varies, too, from the high peaks of the Andes to the flat grassland plains and the low-lying Amazon basin. With so many different conditions, the continent has an extraordinary variety of environments. In Venezuela, great grassland plains known as *llanos* cover one-third of the country. Along the northern tropical coast, are coral reefs and vast sand dunes. In the east, highlands give way to the rain forest of the Amazon basin. Meanwhile in the west, snow covers the high peaks of the Andes mountain range.

Sand dunes in Coro, Venezuela.

During the wet season, between January and March, the Amazon River rises by 65 feet (20 m) and floods an area the size of the state of Iowa.

THE AMAZING AMAZON

Lying near the equator, plants and trees grow all year round in the Amazon basin, making it the world's largest area of tropical rain forest. Many parts of this rain forest remain untouched by human activities, and scientists believe that it may contain up to twenty thousand undiscovered plant species.

Some areas of the Amazon basin receive more than 236 inches (6,000 millimeters) of rainfall per year, but there is plenty of sunshine, too. These year-round hot, wet conditions speed up the rate at which nutrients are released from the dead plants

rotting on the forest floor. Trees quickly absorb the nutrients through their roots and reuse them. Thanks to this rapid cycle of decay and growth, trees in the Amazon can climb to amazing heights even though the soils are of poor quality. This incredible environment also boasts the greatest variety of plant species to be found anywhere on Earth.

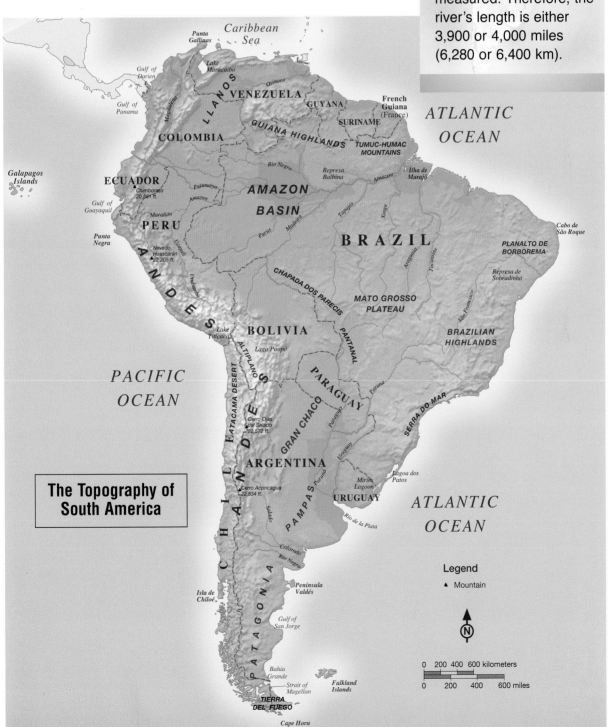

The Topography of South America

Legend

▲ Mountain

0   200 400 600 kilometers

0   200   400   600 miles

15

RAIN FORESTS OF THE SEA

The tropical waters along the continent's Caribbean coast are home to millions of tiny aquatic animals called polyps, which join together to form vast coral reefs. These reefs are sometimes called "the rain forests of the sea" because of the thousands of sea creatures that live on them. Coral reefs are very delicate. Some corals will die just from being touched. Changes in water temperature and murky water can also kill coral, turning an underwater paradise into a dull wasteland. Along Colombia's coast, fishermen have added to the problem by overfishing the waters around the coral reefs. To prevent further damage, the Tayrona National Park extends 115 square miles (479 square kilometers) into the sea. Rangers and scientists regularly monitor the reefs' health.

FACT FILE

Before the formation of the Andes Mountains, the Amazon River drained into the Pacific Ocean rather than flowing east to the Atlantic Ocean, as it does today.

MIGHTY MOUNTAINS

Many of the continent's environments are influenced by the Andes. This immense mountain range began forming sixty million years ago when the Nasca plate beneath the Pacific Ocean was forced beneath the South America plate, pushing the land upward. Towering to a height of 22,834 feet (6,960 m), Mount Aconcagua in Argentina is the highest mountain outside Asia. Parts of the Andes range are still

El Misti, a beautiful snow-capped mountain, towers over the city of Arequipa in Peru.

The *Tren de la Sierra*, or "Mountain Train," climbs from Lima, Peru's capital at sea level, up into the Andes. In the Andes, the train reaches an altitude of 15,844 feet (4,829 m), which is half the height of Mount Everest. At this altitude, the air has 40 percent less oxygen than at sea level, which partly explains why the railway took so long to build. Starting in 1869, and facing great hardship and danger, railway workers carved sixty-six tunnels through the mountains and built fifty-nine bridges over land that is prone to floods and landslides. About two thousand workers died before the railway was completed in 1908.

growing because Earth's plates continue to collide. Movements of the plates force molten rock up to the surface, making some mountains into active volcanoes.

FORESTS IN THE MIST

The warmth of the tropics enables trees to grow high on mountain slopes, at altitudes of up to 10,000 feet (3,000 m). Often cloaked in mist, these "cloud forests" receive 236 inches (6,000 mm) of rain a year. Cloud forests are magical places.

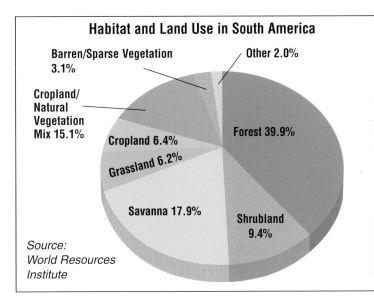

Habitat and Land Use in South America

Barren/Sparse Vegetation 3.1%
Other 2.0%
Cropland/Natural Vegetation Mix 15.1%
Cropland 6.4%
Grassland 6.2%
Forest 39.9%
Savanna 17.9%
Shrubland 9.4%

Source: World Resources Institute

Almost every hillside has its own special plants and animals. Tree trunks are gnarled and stunted by the rain, sun, and mountain winds, and the forest is rich with mosses and ferns. Rotting leaves collect on tree branches. As they break down, they make a kind of soil that provides food for epiphytes. These plants create a hanging garden in the trees, attracting both beautiful hummingbirds in need of nectar and thousands of insects.

Epiphytes in a cloud forest on Mount Cotopaxi, Ecuador. Mount Cotopaxi lies almost on the equator. Yet at 19,393 feet (5,911 m) high, it is always covered with snow. Cotopaxi is also the highest active volcano in the world.

FACT FILE

The Amazon is the world's largest river. It discharges an average of 7,100,000 cubic feet (200,000 cubic meters) of water per second.

SAILING UP THE RIVER

Although the Amazon River originates from water gushing down the steep slopes of the Andes, the rest of the river's path to the sea winds across the low-lying Amazon basin. Large boats can sail 1,000 miles (1,600 km) up the river to the Brazilian city of Manaus because Manaus is only 100 feet (30 m) higher than the mouth of the Amazon.

QUAKES AND TSUNAMIS

In South America, there are many hazards to human life. Even the ground people walk on holds dangers beneath it. Pressure can build up between the plates of Earth's crust as they grind together beneath the continent. When this pressure is released, shock waves radiate outward in the form of an earthquake.

In June 2001, a major earthquake, registering 8.1 on the Richter scale, struck Arequipa, Peru's second-largest city. The city shook for more than one minute, and the tremors were felt hundreds of miles away. About one hundred people died, and thousands more were injured. The earthquake also damaged three-quarters of Arequipa's buildings, including its historic cathedral. Along the coast, towns and villages were hit by a tsunami whipped up by the earthquake, and ocean water surged 2,600 feet (800 m) inland.

A resident of Arequipa steps over the debris left after an earthquake struck in 2001.

EL NIÑO

The weather can bring dangers, too. In the nineteenth century, Peruvian fishermen noticed that about every five years their Pacific fishing waters were unusually warm. This change in climate was named *El Niño*, or "the Christ child," because it normally occurred around Christmas. Scientists are still puzzled by El Niño, but they think it starts when there is a change in the interaction between ocean waters and the atmosphere. In an El Niño year, trade winds are not strong enough to pull the warm waters away from South America's coast. Instead, warm air and ocean currents, flowing from west to east, stop the cooler water of the Peru, or Humboldt, ocean current from reaching the surface.

El Niño is bad news for fishermen. The water is too warm for the anchovies and sardines they normally catch. The warmer ocean also triggers torrential rains that flood coastal towns and villages in southern Peru. During the February 2003 El Niño, a deluge of rain destroyed fields of crops and six thousand homes and killed eighteen people. Stagnant pools of water left behind by the floods and the warmer temperatures also created a breeding ground for mosquitoes that carried diseases like malaria. Nevertheless, this El Niño was weaker than the previous one. In 1997–1998, the strongest El Niño on record killed more than two hundred people in floods and landslides and caused estimated damages of over US$3.5 billion dollars.

Rescue teams sift through rock and mud that buried homes in the village of Mistrato, about 155 miles (250 km) northwest of Bogota, Colombia, after torrential rains caused a mudslide in 2003.

A LOST WORLD

In an area of southeast Venezuela only accessible by air or river, forty flat-topped mountains rise out of the dense rain forest. Native people believed that these *tepuis,* or "table top mountains," were the seats of the gods. The tepuis, made from hard-wearing sandstone and part of an ancient rock formation called the Guiana Highlands, are up to 400 million years old. Back then, South America and the other continents were all part of one gigantic landmass called Gondwanaland. Plunging 3,212 feet (979 m) down the vertical walls of a tepuis is a waterfall named after Jimmy Angel, an American pilot who first spotted it from the air in 1935. Angel Falls is the world's highest uninterrupted waterfall, fifteen times higher than Niagara Falls. Much of this beautiful wilderness is now protected as part of Canaima National Park. Spread over 7 million acres (3 million hectares), Canaima is the third-largest national park in the world.

Venezuela's Angel Falls is the highest waterfall in the world.

FACT FILE

In some parts of the Atacama Desert, no rainfall has ever been recorded.

HIGH AND DRY

The Peru ocean current brings both cold water and air northward, which stops rain clouds from developing over the Atacama Desert. As a result, sometimes it does not rain there for years. The chilly air also cools the desert's temperatures to a maximum of 75° Fahrenheit (24° Celsius).

Part of the Atacama Desert rises to high altitudes. The *altiplano,* or high plain, is one of the most hostile environments on Earth. Because the air is too thin to retain heat, temperatures can drop to –13° F (–25° C) at night. On the altiplano, salt lakes form as meltwater and dissolved salts wash off the mountains. During the day, the water evaporates, leaving behind the salty deposits. In winter, some salt lakes freeze.

THE WORLD'S END

Beyond the grasslands of Argentina and Paraguay is an icy wilderness. Here in Patagonia, the Great Southern Icefield covers 4,400 square miles (11,300 sq km), the biggest expanse of ice outside the Poles. In Patagonia, ferocious storms—with hurricane-force winds and hailstones the size of golf balls—are a risk, even in summer. Glaciers jut out like fingers from the edge of the icefield and act like rivers of ice. As more ice is formed, the glaciers move very slowly, scouring and stripping the mountains in their paths. In recent years, however, some glaciers have actually started shrinking as global climate change has brought warmer temperatures to Patagonia.

The Salar de Uyuni, on Bolivia's altiplano, is the highest and largest salt lake in the world. Here, people mine the salt at 12,000 feet (3,660 m) above sea level. This spectacular lake also attracts many tourists.

Perito Moreno glacier, Patagonia. As parts of the glacier melt, huge chunks of this 164-foot- (50-m-) high wall of ice break off and crash into the lake.

3. THE PEOPLE OF SOUTH AMERICA

When Europeans first came to South America in the 1500s, about two million indigenous people were living in the Amazon rain forest. Each group had developed its own way of life and set of beliefs. Although 170 different languages are still spoken in the Amazon basin, fewer than one million Native people are left in the rain forest, and many groups face extinction.

In 2003, the remaining three hundred Awá people who live in Brazil's Amazon rain forest finally won the rights to their lands after a twenty-year struggle with the Brazilian government.

Elsewhere in South America, other Native groups have disappeared. In Tierra del Fuego, on the southernmost tip of the continent, Indians used to hunt game on the barren plains. Then in 1877, an English trader named Henry Reynard introduced sheep to the area. Tensions grew because the Natives found it easier to hunt the farmers' sheep than hunt wild game. Many Native people were killed in revenge, while others died from diseases that had been introduced by the Europeans. Around 40 percent of the Nukak, an indigenous group in the Colombian Amazon, have died from respiratory diseases, such as flu and tuberculosis.

A RIGHT TO LAND

Without laws to guarantee Native land rights, loggers, ranchers, and new settlers are still taking over territory that has been home to indigenous groups for generations. The Nukak, however, have been more fortunate. They have been given the land rights to their territory in Colombia, protecting their livelihood for the future.

The Aymara and Pacha Mama

Peru, Bolivia, and Ecuador are home to the biggest populations of Native groups, including the Aymara. Although they were previously dominated by the Incas and then the Spanish, the Aymara have retained their own culture and language and are now self-governed. They still live on the high, barren plains of the altiplano on the shores of Lake Titicaca in Peru and Bolivia.

Like most Native people, the Aymara believe that they belong to the land and what they take from the environment should be repaid in some way. According to the Aymara, Pacha Mama ("Mother Earth") helps crops and animals grow. At certain times, they thank Pacha Mama with offerings of coca leaves and animal fat and by sprinkling a type of alcohol on the ground.

An Aymara woman in Bolivia weaves brightly colored cloth. With a population of about fourteen million in Peru, Bolivia, and Ecuador, the Aymara are the largest Native group in South America. The Aymara are descendants of people who were once ruled by the Incas.

FACT FILE

South of the Amazon basin, seventeen Ayoreo people emerged from the forests of Paraguay and made contact with the outside world for the first time in March 2004. They had been forced out of the forest after their precious water holes and much of their land was illegally taken by ranchers and other farmers.

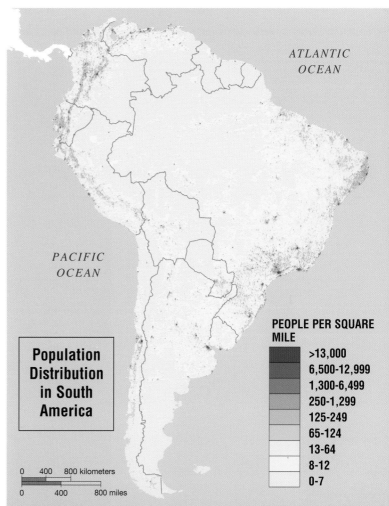

ATLANTIC OCEAN

PACIFIC OCEAN

Population Distribution in South America

PEOPLE PER SQUARE MILE

	>13,000
	6,500-12,999
	1,300-6,499
	250-1,299
	125-249
	65-124
	13-64
	8-12
	0-7

0   400   800 kilometers

0   400   800 miles

MIXED BACKGROUNDS

Relationships between Spanish and indigenous people were widespread in colonial times, and many South Americans today are *mestizo,* or of mixed Indian and Spanish ancestry. Other South Americans are descendants of West African slaves.

People in Suriname have an extraordinary variety of backgrounds. Some can trace their roots back to West Africa and Indonesia, as descendants of slaves brought over by the British or Dutch. Hindustanis make up one-third of Suriname's population. They first came from northern India in the late 1800s. By this time, slavery had been abolished, and Hindustanis came to work on Suriname's plantations in return for food, clothes, and shelter. After centuries of intermarriage, one-third of Suriname's people are Creole, with both black and white ancestry.

FACT FILE

The family of Alberto Fujimori, who was Peru's president from 1990 to 2000, originally came from Japan. Thousands of Brazilians also have Japanese heritage.

A Guaraní man and child hold crosses as part of a religious ceremony in Paraguay.

● ● ● ▶ IN FOCUS:
Spanish/Guarani

Unlike other South Americans, Paraguayans kept their local language, Guaraní, during colonial times. Visiting missionaries from Europe grew fond of the sound of Guaraní, and intermarriage between local people and the Spanish was widespread. Today, most Paraguayans can speak both Spanish and Guaraní.

rgentina's population is almost entirely European origin. About three million alians moved to Argentina in the late neteenth and early twentieth centuries, ong with people from other parts of urope. Smaller groups of immigrants ttled there, too. In the mountainous rovince of Chubut, Welsh was the cond language until the 1990s.

auchos are the cowboys of Argentina, lmired for their courage, self-reliance, d love of the land. With their silver urs, horses, and packs of dogs, gauchos ill herd their livestock on *estancias*, or nches, scattered across Argentina's assland plains.

Many of Argentina's gauchos still wear black Spanish hats and Indian shawls, representing their mixed Indian and Spanish background.

SLAND LIFE

bout 300 miles (483 km) off the coast f Argentina, people on the Falkland lands (or Las Malvinas, as they are nown in Argentina) speak English and rn a living from fishing, sheep farming, d oil exploration. Despite Argentina's ttempt to seize control of the islands in e 1982 Falklands War, they have emained under British control since 833. In many ways, Falkland Islanders ave more in common with Britain than ith the rest of South America. Today, early half the islands' residents are ritish troops protecting the islands.

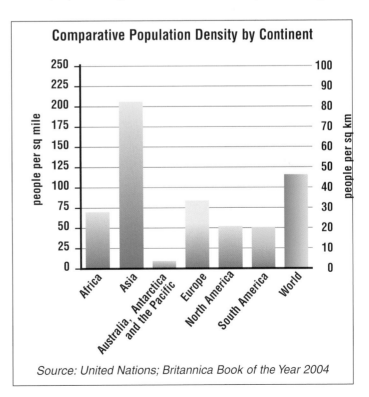

Comparative Population Density by Continent

Source: United Nations; Britannica Book of the Year 2004

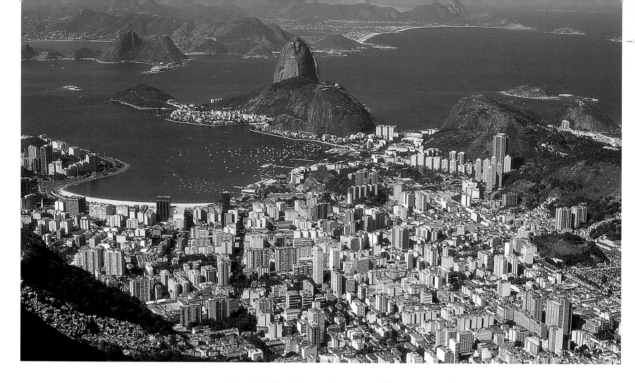

From 1763 until 1960, Rio de Janeiro was Brazil's capital city. Due to its beautiful setting, Rio's residents often call it "The Marvellous City."

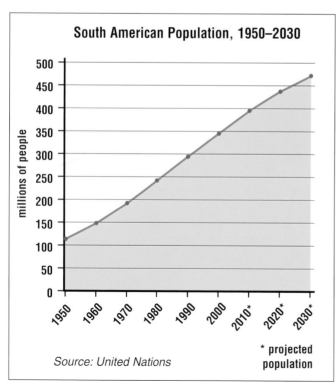

South American Population, 1950–2030

Source: United Nations

* projected population

In 1900, about forty million people lived in South America, and the population growth rate was high. Many men wanted large families as a sign of status, and farming families needed children to work the land. At the same time, large numbers of people moved from Europe to make a new start in South America. Although birth rates have since slowed, the total population of the continent today is nearly ten times greater than it was one hundred years ago. The majority of people now live in towns and cities, much like in industrialized countries. Many people have left a life of poverty in the rural areas and moved to cities in search of a better standard of living. Population growth within the cities themselves has added to urban sprawl. Nevertheless, many South Americans find it difficult to make a living, and poverty puts great stress on families.

The growth of cities has led to environmental problems that affect all South Americans. In Santiago, Chile, the five million residents must cope with one of the highest levels of air pollution in the world. Smoke, gases, and other particles in the air become trapped like a blanket over the city; and more than one million cars spew out pollutants, adding to the problem. Many people suffer from illnesses caused by pollution, and city authorities are now taking action to clean up the city. They have introduced buses that run on cleaner fuels, and on days when pollution levels are particularly high, the city authorities order factories to close.

FACT FILE

More than 80 percent of Brazilians and nearly 90 percent of Argentinians live in towns and cities. Brazil has fifteen cities that are home to more than one million residents each. More than fifteen million people live in the Brazilian city of São Paolo alone.

IN FOCUS: A boost for the *favelas*

In Rio de Janeiro, one-fifth of the residents live in poor neighborhoods, called *favelas*, scattered around the city on waste ground or on one of Rio's many steep ravines. Over the last decade, city authorities have invested in a program called the "Favela Bairio" to create a better quality of life for these residents. In one neighborhood, Villa Canoas, a new sewage system and waste collection service has reduced the risk of disease, particularly among children. Educational facilities have improved, too, with a new community school and a training center for adults.

Building on the skills and strong community spirit among Villa Canoas residents, a program has helped new businesses flourish, such as this locally run company that makes apple strudel.

Many families move to towns and cities so their children can go to better schools. Yet poverty often forces the children to earn money for the family instead. Across South America, school drop-out rates are so high that the average time spent at school of five years may be less than it is in poorer areas of Africa. Primary education is free in Brazil, yet nearly one-fifth of Brazilians cannot read or write. With fewer educated people, finding well-qualified teachers to work in schools becomes more difficult, and the gap between rich people qualified for well-paid jobs and those without an education continues to grow.

LIFE ON THE STREET

Many children living on the streets of cities, such as Rio de Janeiro, Brazil, have never been to school. For some, the streets are a workplace where they earn money to support the rest of the family. For others, the streets are their home, day and night. Some have run away from home because of a breakdown in their families or because they have suffered violence and abuse. Street children must learn to fend for themselves, because their lives can be difficult and dangerous. Like all children, however, street children have rights, and they need help to find safe, legal ways of looking after themselves. An organization called Cruzada do Menor (Children's Crusade) has set up a center where street children can learn how to read

These homeless children, who live on the street in Brazil, are looking for food or things to sell.

and write and gain other skills that will improve their chances of getting decent jobs in the city.

HEALTH MATTERS

Although other continents, such as Africa, have more people living with HIV/AIDS, the problem is growing in South America. Doctors think there may be two thousand street children who are HIV-positive in Rio alone. Yet Brazil has also become an example to the world in its fight

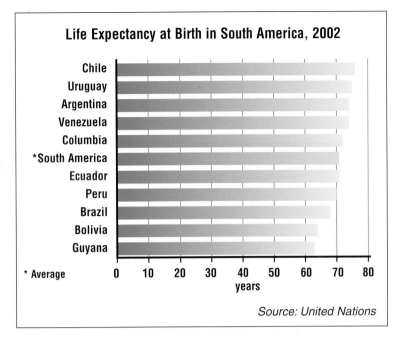

Life Expectancy at Birth in South America, 2002

Chile
Uruguay
Argentina
Venezuela
Columbia
*South America
Ecuador
Peru
Brazil
Bolivia
Guyana

* Average   0   10   20   30   40   50   60   70   80
years

Source: United Nations

against HIV/AIDS. Thanks to a widespread education program, Brazilians are more likely to know how to avoid infection. Most Brazilians are Catholic, but even though the traditional teachings of the Catholic Church are against the use of contraceptives, condoms are widely used in Brazil. At the same time, drugs used to suppress the symptoms of HIV/AIDS are virtually free. These drugs are made locally by Brazilian companies and are cheaper than equivalent drugs sold on the international market.

South American teenagers are being educated about the dangers of sexually transmitted diseases, including HIV and AIDS.

FACT FILE

Adults living with HIV/AIDS in Brazil make up 0.7 percent of the population, compared to 20.1 percent in South Africa.

4. SOUTH AMERICAN CULTURE AND RELIGION

*T*ODAY, MORE THAN 80 PERCENT OF SOUTH AMERICANS ARE PRACTICING Catholics. During colonial times, missionaries from Spain and Portugal came to convert indigenous people to Christianity. They traveled far and wide, sometimes learning Native languages in order to explain their faith more easily. Despite the missionaries' efforts, however, many Native groups have kept their own ancient beliefs. In Chile, for example, the Mapuche people believe that bad luck, disease, and death come from evil magic. Healers, called *machi*, hold special ceremonies to guard against these evils.

MIXING RELIGIONS

In some parts of the continent, Catholicism has been mixed with other beliefs to form a new religion. In Bahia state, Brazil, Candomblé combines Catholicism with traditional Indian customs as well as African beliefs that were brought to South America by slaves. A Candomblé ceremony is led by a priest or priestess and may last for several hours. The people call on their gods to possess them by performing dances and songs to the beat of an African drum. The dancers work themselves into a trance, then change into fine costumes and have their bodies painted with intricate patterns. Then, each dancer performs a special dance to please one of the gods.

SEPARATE RELIGIONS

Other peoples have brought their own blend of religion to the continent. In 1927, Mennonites came from Canada to settle in Paraguay. Paraguayans welcomed people from other countries because many men had been killed in wars, and most of the thorny forests and barren

Catholic São Francisco church, in Salvador da Bahia, Brazil.

plains of the Chaco in western Paraguay were uninhabited and unused. Originally from Germany, the Mennonites were strict Protestants. They also had a reputation for being skilled farmers and hard workers. In return for their religious freedom and the right to speak German, the Mennonites agreed to occupy the sweltering Chaco plains. Today, twenty-eight thousand Mennonites live in Paraguay, and they run most of the country's dairy farms.

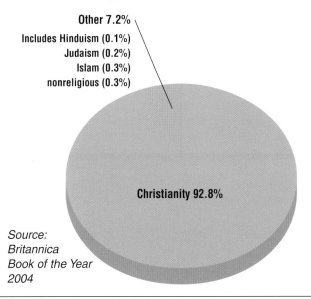

Religions in South America

Other 7.2%
Includes Hinduism (0.1%)
Judaism (0.2%)
Islam (0.3%)
nonreligious (0.3%)

Christianity 92.8%

Source:
Britannica
Book of the Year
2004

• • • • • • ▶ IN FOCUS: The Day of the Dead

For the Aymara in Peru, November 2 is a very important day. They believe this is the time when the spirits of the dead visit the living. Aymara families prepare breads in different shapes and decorate tombs with sweets, flowers, onions, and sugarcane.

The Aymara believe that these gifts will help the spirits of their dead relatives find their way into new bodies so that they may be reincarnated, or reborn.

Aymara Day of the Dead celebration in Bolivia.

People in every corner of Brazil celebrate Carnivale, and each carnivale has its own rhythms, dances, and styles.

LET'S RUMBA!

Rumba means "party" to most South American people. Across the continent, parties are big, loud, and a lot of fun. In Brazil, the biggest party of all happens each year just before Lent. *Carnivale* takes place on the streets of every Brazilian city. For five days and nights, the streets are filled with people in colorful costumes, dancing to a samba beat.

In many poor neighborhoods, young people practice for months at samba schools in order to be the best samba troupe. But in Rio de Janeiro, many young people dance to funk music rather than samba these days. Originating in Brazil, funk mixes rap, techno beats, and thudding bass lines.

Meanwhile, at Colombian parties, hips sway to the rhythm of *cumbia*, which has both local and African influences. The shuffling footwork of cumbia dancing may hark back to the time when African slaves tried to dance with chains around their ankles. Modern cumbia adds hip-hop to the mix, giving it new life and fans.

LET'S ROCK!

Many young Brazilians and Argentinians are huge rock fans, too. In January, Rio de Janeiro stages the "Rock in Rio" festival, one of the biggest rock concerts in the world, where people flock to see both local and international musicians. In 1985, the first Rock in Rio festival, following years of military rule in Brazil, was seen as a celebration of freedom.

FOOTBALL CRAZY

South Americans are passionate about soccer. In Brazil, many people take the day off if the national team is playing. If they score, fireworks light up the sky in many Brazilian cities. The atmosphere is more like a big party—so long as the home team wins. When the Colombian team lost to the United States and crashed out of the 1994 World Cup, for example, the picture was very different. Colombian defender Andres Escobar scored in his own goal and was blamed for the team's defeat. Ten days later, he was murdered in Medellín, his hometown. Escobar's murder remains unsolved, but many believe that one of the drug cartels was responsible. They had lost millions of dollars on bets because of Colombia's early exit from the competition.

Colombian soccer fans cheer for their team during the Copa América, the oldest national soccer tournament in the world. Since 1916, there have been forty-one tournaments. Soccer teams representing countries across the Americas battle it out for the prized trophy. The greatest victors are Argentina and Uruguay—they have won the tournament fourteen times each!

STORIES OF MAGICAL REALISM

Some South American authors are famous for their colorful, dreamlike stories. This type of writing is known as *magical realism*. Nobel prize-winning author Gabriel García Márquez has been influenced by the way in which his grandmother used to tell him stories. Márquez's first book about his own childhood in Aracataca, in northern Colombia, called *Living to Tell the Tale*, became a best-selling book in the Spanish-speaking world. Another popular magical realist writer is Isabel Allende. She grew up in Chile, and her uncle, Salvador Allende, was president until he was murdered in 1973. She has lived in the United States since the late 1980s, and her books have been translated into nearly thirty different languages.

WHAT'S COOKING?

A favorite dish in the coastal communities of Peru and Ecuador is *ceviche*, made from raw white fish marinated in lemon juice, onions, and hot peppers. Traditionally, ceviche was served with corn-on-the-cob, but today many Ecuadorians prefer it with a bowl of popcorn.

A plate of *ceviche*, served with roasted corn kernels and popcorn.

Food is bought and traded at local markets. At Saquisili market in Ecuador, farmers come down from the mountain slopes to trade vegetables for bananas, pigs, cloth, or even a few llamas. Market days are also a chance to meet friends and catch up on local gossip.

South Americans are avid meat eaters, too. People in Argentina and Uruguay are proud of their succulent beef steaks, which are often cooked slowly over an open fire. In the highlands of Peru, people still eat roast guinea pig, a delicacy since Inca times. Food in Brazil is steeped in history as well, as it draws on the different backgrounds of the country's people. In Bahia state, *acarajés* are one of the tastiest items on the menu. These spicy snacks use ingredients, such as palm oil, prawns, and peppers, celebrating the people's West African ancestry.

These colorful rugs and wall hangings are on sale at a market in Otoválo, Ecuador.

A CUP OF TEA

Many South Americans enjoy *maté*, a kind of tea made from a wild plant. The Guaraní people in Paraguay have been drinking maté for thousands of years. In the past, they believed that maté held magic powers. People still take a break with a cup of maté in modern-day Paraguay. They drink it through a silver straw, from a small, polished gourd, passing it around to share with family or friends.

5. NATURAL RESOURCES IN SOUTH AMERICA

MOST SOUTH AMERICAN COUNTRIES HAVE PLENTIFUL SUPPLIES OF minerals and precious metals. Chile is the world's leading producer of copper, and the country has rich reserves of other resources, such as lithium, nitrates, and iron ore. Chuquicamata, in northern Chile, about 155 miles (250 km) from Antofagasta, is the largest copper mine in the world. Mining and smelting copper, however, releases large amounts of pollution into the air and water, which threatens the health of many Chileans. Chuqicamata was once shut down for an entire month because of the extent of the pollution the mine produced.

NEW DISCOVERIES

Bolivia is also rich in natural resources. In 1544, an Indian named Diego Huallpa discovered an enormous supply of silver on the altiplano, 13,000 feet (4,000 m) above sea level. For the next two hundred years, the Spanish rulers of Bolivia took most of these riches back to Spain. Tin became another source of wealth for Bolivia. But in the 1980s, the electronics industry, which bought tin, was depressed, and less tin was needed. In 1985, world tin prices collapsed, many tin mines closed down, and thousands of Bolivians lost their jobs.

A miner in Potosi, Bolivia, is shown mining silver in Cerro Rico (Rich Mountain).

FACT FILE

Between 1545 and 1660, the Spanish took about 16 million tons (14 million tonnes) of Bolivia's silver back to Spain.

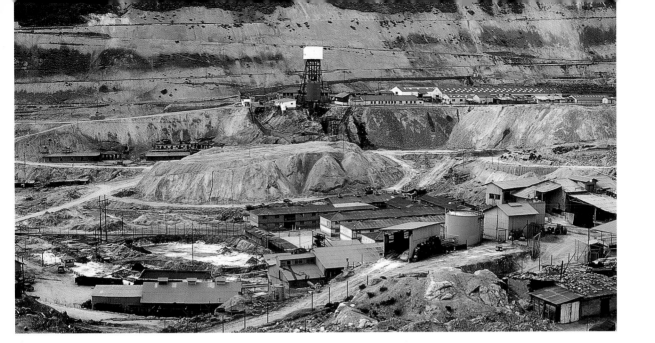

RUMORS OF RICHES

Argentina means "the Land of Silver" in Latin, but this country's rich farmland is a much more important resource than its precious metals. The name came from the first Spanish explorers, who reached the country in the early 1500s. When they were shipwrecked at the mouth of the Rio de la Plata (Silver River), they were greeted by Indians who presented them with silver objects. By 1524, a rumor reached Spain that Argentina had a mountain rich in silver, and many more Spaniards sailed over to find their fortune. They were disappointed, however, to discover that the story was just a local legend.

Other valuable resources lie beneath the Amazon rain forest. At Carajás, the world's largest source of iron ore was discovered when a plane flew over the Brazilian Amazon, and the pilot saw a giant red gap in the surrounding green carpet of forest. Since then, trains up to 1 mile (2 km) long have transported the ore out of Carajás, and the vast Tucuruí dam has been built to power its iron-smelting furnaces. The artificial lake behind the dam is bigger than some European countries.

This lead mine in the Andes is near La Oroya, in central Peru.

FACT FILE

Gold was the first metal to be used by people in South America—possibly as long ago as 2000 B.C. in Peru. Today, more than one million miners, known as *garimpeiros*, still come to the Amazon basin in search of gold.

An oil pipeline in the rain forest of Ecuador, near Lago Agrio.

BLACK GOLD

Energy resources, such as natural gas and oil, are also very important in South America. Venezuelan oil fields around Lake Maracaibo account for most of that country's export earnings, with Venezuela providing 13 percent of the oil imported by the United States. Ecuador relies on oil for more than one-third of its export earnings, after rich deposits were discovered beneath the Amazon rain forest in 1967. The oil is pumped across the Andes, through the Trans-Andean pipeline, to the port of Esmeraldas in the west.

POWER FROM THE AMAZON

The Amazon region is the source of another type of energy—hydro-electric power (HEP), derived from fast-flowing water. Unlike burning oil or coal, HEP does not release harmful gases into the atmosphere. Plus, as long as there is running water, this type of power will not run out. Dams are built to trap the water's energy. Brazil has six hundred large dams, but they have been criticized by environmental groups. When a river is dammed, the flooding behind the dam can destroy houses and farmland, and the still water creates a breeding ground for mosquitoes. Many people must leave their homes, and very few of them receive compensation.

On the Paraguay–Brazil border, the vast Itaipu dam is currently the world's biggest HEP project. A joint venture between Paraguay and Brazil, the dam harnesses the power of the Paraná River and generates enough energy for nearly all of Paraguay's electricity.

The Itaipu dam is 5 miles (8 km) long, and it has created a lake or reservoir that covers 870 square miles (1,400 sq km).

•••••▶ IN FOCUS: Selling off Bolivia's assets

Since 1993, with crushing debts and few other ways of making money, the Bolivian government has been selling off the country's natural resources to overseas companies. Many Bolivians, however, are very reluctant to give up these resources. In Cochabamba, angry residents clashed with police after the government sold the city's water system to foreign owners in 1999. Water bills more than doubled, and people reacted by organizing protest marches and a four-day strike. The government later cancelled the contract. In 2003, protests broke out across Bolivia over plans to pump the country's natural gas to Mexico and the United States. Many people believed that the gas revenues would only line the pockets of a few, mostly foreign investors, while most Bolivians would not benefit at all. The protests forced the President of Bolivia, Gonzalo Sanchez de Lozada, to resign in 2003.

A group of Kayapó people gather at Altamira, Brazil, in 1989 to voice opposition to the proposed dam.

As South America's fastest-growing consumer of energy, Chile has also been investing in HEP. Chileans have been building dams to trap the wild meltwater rivers that run off the slopes of the Andes. But like the Brazilians who live along the dammed tributaries of the Amazon, life for the people of Chile who live along these rivers is changing irreversibly. Meanwhile, some Native people in Brazil have been joining forces with environmentalists and human rights activists to fight back against the building of dams.

In February 1989, the Kayapó people gathered at Altamira in the Brazilian Amazon to protest against a massive dam-building project along the Xingu river. Their campaign won worldwide support, and the project was abandoned. Had it been built, the dam would have flooded many of the Kayapó's sacred lands.

THE RUBBER INDUSTRY

Rubber used to be an important resource from the Amazon rain forest. When a cut is made in the trunk of a rubber tree, a sticky liquid called latex oozes out. Latex is the source of natural rubber. Boosted by the invention of the rubber tire and the development of steamboats for transportation up the river, the rubber industry boomed in the 1800s when nearly all the rubber used worldwide came from the Amazon region. Then, the British took seeds to Southeast Asia to plant vast numbers of rubber trees, and the Amazon's rubber industry collapsed. Nevertheless, by working together in cooperatives, some people still make a living from rubber-tapping.

THE TIMBER TRADE

Timber is another important resource. Thanks to Chile's fertile soil, pine trees grow faster here than in other countries. In tropical areas, hardwoods, such as mahogany, sell for a high price on the world market.

Trade in tropical hardwoods is nothing new. About five hundred years ago, indigenous people in the Amazon rain forest traded with Europeans, exchanging mahogany for axes, mirrors, and colored beads. The timber trade, however, has since spiraled out of control. To meet the high demand for tropical hardwoods in rich countries, loggers destroy large areas of rain forest in search of this precious timber. New networks of roads carve through the rain forest to reach the timber more easily. In addition, by creating new openings into the forest, these roads encourage more settlers to try their luck in the Amazon, destroying even more forest.

The Atlantic forest along Brazil's coastline is nearly gone because people have cleared the land to build houses, grow crops, or use the trees as timber.

6. The South American Economy

One hundred years ago, Argentina's plains were opened up for cattle ranching on a massive scale. Argentina became, by far, the richest country in South America. Thousands of poorer Europeans came in search of work on the ranches. During World Wars I and II, Argentina and neighboring Uruguay exported tinned beef in vast quantities to feed hungry people in war-torn Europe. Virtually any crop can be grown in Argentina, thanks to its varied climate that stretches from the tropics to the Antarctic waters. Argentina is now the world's fifth-biggest exporter of farm products.

GM Conflict

One of Argentina's most important crops is soybeans. Many Argentinian farmers use genetically modified (GM) soybean seeds that can be grown all year round. Until September 2003,

Ranch hands rounding up cattle in Argentina.

GM crops were banned across Brazil because of concerns that their pollen or seeds might escape and contaminate other varieties. Some Brazilian farmers also fear that GM crops may increase their dependence on the multinational companies that make and sell the seeds. But GM seeds have already been smuggled into Brazil, contaminating other fields and angering many Brazilians.

• • • • • • ▶ IN FOCUS: Dollar bananas

Ecuador is the world's largest exporter of bananas. About one-quarter of the bananas eaten in the United States and one-fifth of those eaten in Europe come from Ecuador. Ecuadorian bananas are sometimes called "dollar bananas" because they are very cheap. One reason for their low price is that laborers—some of them children—work long hours for very low wages on Ecuador's vast plantations.

Multinational companies own many of the plantations. To produce as many bananas as possible, some of the companies use a lot of chemicals to kill insect pests and make the bananas grow faster. These chemicals, however, can pollute the environment and may cause health problems.

Plantation workers are at particular risk. Some have no protective clothing, even though the chemicals can cause cancer and infertility. Fortunately, some companies, both large corporations and small farming cooperatives linked to Fair Trade

programs, are now starting to grow bananas in ways that are less harmful to the environment, using fewer chemicals and recycling waste.

Bananas grown in Ecuador are labeled for sale in the United States and other countries abroad.

43

FACT FILE

The biggest oil field found in the Americas since 1969 was opened in Colombia's Cuisiana basin, east of Bogotá, in 1994.

Most of Colombia's coffee is grown on small, family-run farms. The farmers rely on workers to handpick the coffee beans, rather than use machines.

CHANGING WORLD PRICES

In addition to farm products, raw materials known as primary products are also important to South American economies. Oil dominates the economies of Venezuela, Ecuador, and Colombia, while Chile depends on sales of copper for half its wealth.

When prices fall on the world market, countries that rely on selling these primary products can find themselves in trouble. When copper prices plummeted in the late 1990s, unemployment and debt rose in Chile. Since then, rising copper prices have improved the fortunes of some people in Chile. Colombia's 560,000 coffee farmers have had a tougher time. With more countries producing coffee worldwide, prices have plunged to an all-time low. Many coffee farmers in Colombia have decided to give up altogether. Others are joining together to grow Fair Trade coffee, for which producers are paid a higher, fairer price. Fair Trade coffee farmers in Colombia use the extra money to improve their farms and invest in better health and education services for their communities.

Unlike its neighbors, Brazil no longer relies on selling primary products. Instead, it has expanded its manufacturing industries. Since the 1950s, Brazilians have opened their own factories to take advantage of new markets in Europe, the United States, and neighboring Argentina. Today, one-quarter of Brazilians work in manufacturing, and many multinational companies have chosen to locate factories there. Brazil is now one of the world's largest producers of steel, cars, and petrochemicals. It is also a big exporter of TV programs to Europe, Africa, and China. With a mixed economy, Brazil is better able to withstand changes in an international marketplace. As a result, it makes more money than any other South American country, and it had the thirteenth-largest economy in the world in 2003.

Bolivia is the continent's poorest country. Two-thirds of its population live in poverty, and the country has the highest infant mortality rate in South America. Without direct access to the sea, Bolivians have to pay more to export and import goods. These additional charges increase the cost of Bolivian goods and make them less attractive to buyers.

FACT FILE

Coffee is a major South American export. Brazil is the world's largest coffee producer, while Colombia is the third largest.

Workers at a Chrysler plant in Brazil slowly lower the cab of a Dodge pickup truck.

President Lula da Silva talks to shantytown residents in Recife, northern Brazil, during the launch of an antihunger campaign in January 2003.

FACT FILE

About 80 percent of Brazil's farmland is owned by just 4 percent of the population, and 40 percent of Brazilians live on less than one U.S. dollar a day.

UNEQUAL BENEFITS

For all its newfound wealth, Brazil's riches are not evenly spread. Half its factories are in the southeastern part of the country. In addition, much of Brazil's farmland is owned by a handful of wealthy families, leaving millions without any land at all. In 2002, Lula da Silva was elected as Brazil's president, and he brought new hope to Brazil's poor. Lula was born in the northeast, Brazil's poorest region. As a former shoe-shine boy and metal worker, Lula knows what it is like to be poor. He has promised to make the fight against hunger and poverty the top priority of his presidency.

DANGEROUSLY IN DEBT

Argentina's economic problems have been growing. Some people blame the government for wasting money and giving payoffs to friends and allies. Others blame problems linked to debt. During the 1980s, when interest rates were low, Argentina accepted loan offers from overseas banks to pay for new developments. When rates later rose sharply, Argentina struggled to pay even the interest on the loans, let alone the debt itself.

To improve the situation, foreign banks and governments encouraged Argentina to remove trade barriers, such as taxes on imported goods. With this "free market,"

Argentina was considered more likely to attract foreign investors. The disadvantage, however, was that Argentinian farmers and businesspeople no longer had any protection against foreign competition.

Unlike Brazil, which has an even bigger debt, the Argentinian economy could not grow fast enough to repay its loans. In 2002, Argentina reached a crisis point. Its total debt rose to US$155 billion, and the country was refused any more loans from overseas. Chaos followed. Argentina changed its president five times in eighteen months. Unemployment skyrocketed, health and education services were cut, and one-quarter of the country's children suffered from malnutrition. Meanwhile, Argentina's currency (the peso) fell by 70 percent against the U.S. dollar, and millions of Argentinians watched their hard-earned savings crash in value. For many, this was the last straw, and riots broke out across Buenos Aires, Argentina's capital city. Today, although debt remains a burden, a sense of calm has returned, as ordinary Argentinians try to get on with their lives.

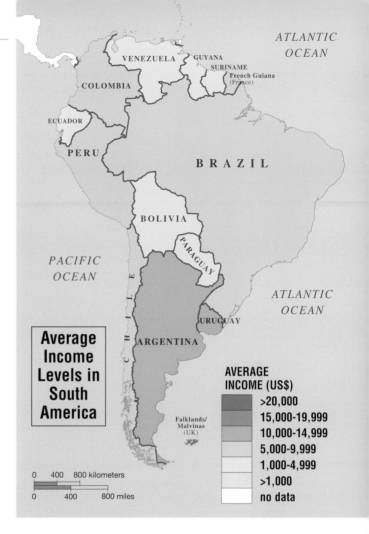

Police carry away a demonstrator on the streets of Buenos Aires during protests in December 2002.

7. SOUTH AMERICA IN THE WORLD

SOUTH AMERICA IS THE ORIGIN OF SOME FOODS THAT PEOPLE IN THE REST of the world now take for granted. For example, potatoes came from the Andes originally and have been farmed there since the time of the Inca in the early 1500s. Potatoes can grow on the steepest mountain slopes and in the thinnest of soils. The Aymara people cultivate as many as four hundred different varieties of potato in the Andes.

A girl picking coca leaves near Quillabamba in Peru. Picking coca leaves is hard, poorly paid work.

For thousands of years, another crop called coca has been grown on the mountain slopes of the Andes. Millions of South Americans still buy coca leaves. They chew it or make coca tea as a remedy for the effects of high altitude or even to ease the pain of childbirth. But coca is also the raw material for cocaine.

DRUGS AND VIOLENCE

The illegal production of cocaine turned a local culture into a multimillion dollar industry, especially in Colombia. Gangsters from Colombian cities, such as Medellín, formed groups known as cartels to control the production of cocaine from coca leaves and its illegal sale to drug users elsewhere. With their vast profits, drug cartels became very powerful. They used violence against competitors and bribed police, politicians, and customs officers to protect their business deals. Although the Colombian authorities had some success in arresting some of the cartel ringleaders, the drug trade remains strong. Today, rebel groups in Colombia control the cocaine trade, and drug trafficking has expanded into neighboring Brazil and Ecuador.

FIGHTING THE DRUG WAR

The U.S. government has been so alarmed by the flow of cocaine into the United States that it has given millions of dollars in aid to Colombia to fight the "drug war." As part of "Plan Colombia," the United States is training and arming Colombian soldiers to fight cocaine dealers and smugglers. To destroy the coca crop, the soldiers spray it with chemicals or burn it, along with the buildings where the coca is processed into cocaine. Although cocaine abuse is a growing problem in South America, many people believe that the real problem lies with drug users in other countries. It is argued that, as long as there is a demand, the drug trade will continue.

An armed soldier hangs out of a helicopter, looking for illegal coca fields in Colombia.

Encouraging coca farmers to grow other crops may be another way of destroying the cocaine trade. Many South American farmers, however, cannot make enough money from other crops. They find it difficult to compete with farmers elsewhere who receive government subsidies, or financial help, to grow crops more cheaply. In Europe and the United States, farmers not only receive subsidies, they are also protected by taxes on imported goods. Meanwhile, farmers in the Andes have no such protection.

A NEW VOICE FOR THE POOR WORLD

To improve conditions in the region, Brazil, Argentina, Uruguay, Paraguay, and Peru joined forces to form Mercosur, a common market where businesses can trade freely without paying extra taxes. The United States wants to create a free trade zone across most of the Americas, but critics argue that, without any protection, South American businesses could never compete with U.S. companies. Instead, Argentina and Brazil are looking at ways to make Mercosur bigger and more powerful.

South American countries, with their neighbors in North and Central America and the Caribbean, are also members of the Organization of American States (OAS), which has its headquarters in Washington, D.C. The thirty-five member countries of the OAS are working together to promote peace and security and to tackle international problems, such as terrorism and the illegal drug trade.

Tourism is becoming an important industry in several South American countries. Growing numbers of South Americans are becoming tourists, too.

As the world's thirteenth-richest country, Brazil has a loud voice on the world stage. Every other year, Brazil holds a massive gathering of people called the "World Social Forum" to share ideas on how to make the world a fairer place. Brazil also works closely with India and South Africa. These big developing countries are pushing for better trading conditions for poorer and less powerful nations.

The World Social Forum opens in Porto Alegre, Brazil.

IN FOCUS: Che Guevara

An Argentinian doctor named Ernesto "Che" Guevara has become a worldwide symbol of idealism and rebellion. As a young man in the 1960s, Che traveled across the continent on his motorcycle and helped rebel movements in Mexico, Guatemala, Bolivia, and Cuba. He first met Fidel Castro, Cuba's president, in Mexico. When Castro seized power in the 1959 Cuban revolution, Che became Castro's chief lieutenant. As president of Cuba's national bank, he was eager to cut ties to the United States because he believed it opposed his vision of justice for the poor. In 1967, with the help of the U.S. Central Intelligence Agency (CIA), Bolivian troops captured and killed Che in the Andes.

A banner showing a likeness of Che Guevara is carried during a rally in La Paz, Bolivia, which was held to mark International Labor Day in May 2004.

51

OIL PRODUCERS

As the world's seventh-largest oil producer, Venezuela can flex its muscles internationally as a member of the Organization of Petroleum Exporting Countries (OPEC). Together, OPEC members are able to influence the amount of oil that is pumped into the world marketplace. Through this process, they aim to keep oil prices stable and guarantee themselves a steady income. But, as more countries produce their own oil and alternative energy sources, such as tidal energy, become available, OPEC is losing some of its influence.

SOCCER STARS

The rest of the world has benefited from South America's rich culture, too. Spectators around the world

An Ariane rocket blasts off from the European Space Agency launch site at Kourou, French Guiana, in 2003.

FACT FILE

French Guiana still has strong European links. For example, the European Space Agency launches rockets from French Guiana.

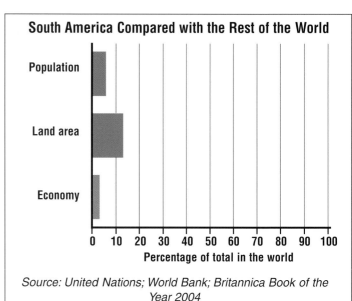

South America Compared with the Rest of the World

Population

Land area

Economy

0 10 20 30 40 50 60 70 80 90 100
Percentage of total in the world

Source: United Nations; World Bank; Britannica Book of the Year 2004

marvel at the skill of South American soccer players. A number of the continent's best players have moved to Europe to earn enormous salaries at top clubs there. Brazil has won the World Cup four times—more often than any other country.

TANGO

Music from South America can be heard all over the world. Tango was created in the slums of Buenos Aires. The first tango dancers were soldiers discharged from the army or immigrants from Italy and Spain who had arrived in the city's port to begin a new life. Lonely and homesick, these young men danced in pairs. With its fast, sensual rhythms, many people were shocked by tango. By the 1920s, however, it was all the rage in Paris and other European cities. Today, tango is experiencing a revival back in its homeland. Young Argentinians are learning the complicated steps from their older relatives.

Tango dancers in Buenos Aires.

IN FOCUS:
Diego Maradona

Diego Maradona was one of the greatest soccer players of all time. Born in a slum in Buenos Aires, he began his career with the Boca Juniors, one of the top clubs in Argentina. After playing for his country in the 1982 World Cup, Maradona moved to Europe, helping both Barcelona and Naples win a string of trophies. In 1986, he captained the Argentina team that went on to win the World Cup. During this championship, Maradona became a soccer legend after he scored an extraordinary goal against England. Many believe it was the best goal in the history of the game.

8. SOUTH AMERICAN WILDLIFE

MORE THAN ONE-THIRD OF THE WORLD'S TEN THOUSAND BIRD SPECIES live in South America. One of the most striking is the keel-billed toucan. The toucan's amazing beak is actually hollow and very light, but it is perfect for cracking open seeds to eat. High in the treetops, toucans use their colorful beaks as flags, throwing their heads from side to side. Their distinctive call can be heard for miles. Meanwhile, millions of insects are busy on the forest floor. Leafcutter ants gather and chew leaves into a pulp, making a bed of fertilizer on which a special fungus grows. Then, the ants consume the fungus as food.

MAKING THE FOREST LAST

People in central Guyana are trying to use their tropical rain forest without destroying the forest itself. Run by local people, the Iwokrama Forest covers a little more than 916,000 acres (371,000 hectares). Half the area has been left undisturbed. The other half has become a center for researchers, working with the Native people who live in the forest. Scientists can study the forest canopy from a new 65-foot- (20-m-) high walkway that has been built between the trees. A growing number of adventurous tourists are visiting Iwokrama, too. Tourism brings in about US$120,000 a year. Much of this money is used to help local villages and to train people as guides.

Toucans don't just eat fruits and berries. Sometimes, they eat small reptiles or the eggs or young of other birds.

FACT FILE

The Amazon basin contains about one-tenth of all known plant, animal, and insect species on Earth.

Piranhas are flesh-eating fish with razor-sharp teeth that live in the Amazon River and its tributaries. Piranhas, however, are not as dangerous as thought—they only attack if they smell blood. Another flesh-eater crouching on the riverbank is the caiman, a member of the alligator family. The Amazon is also home to the piraracu, the world's largest freshwater fish. Although it grows up to 13 feet (4 m) long and weighs as much as 440 pounds (200 kilograms), piraracu can still leap out of the water to grab young birds.

More than ten million caiman alligators live in the Brazilian Pantanal, one of the world's largest wetlands.

ABOVE THE CLOUDS

Soaring majestically above the Andes, with a wingspan of 9 feet (3 m), the condor is the world's largest flying bird. It can glide for up to one hour on mountain air currents. Condors are a kind of vulture, feeding off the remains of dead animals. They use their incredible eyesight to spot food from high in the sky.

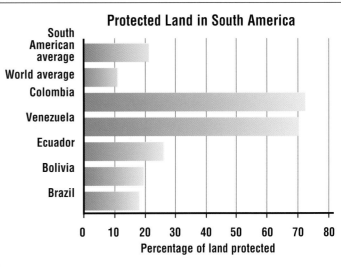

Protected Land in South America

Percentage of land protected

Source: World Resources Institute

Galibi, Suriname, is the largest breeding ground in the world for the endangered giant leatherback turtle. These turtles can grow up to 6 feet (2 m) long and can live to the grand old age of fifty. In 1995, there were about eighteen hundred leatherback turtles and more than six thousand green turtles nesting at Galibi.

GUARDING TURTLES

Along the coast of Suriname, turtles come out of the sea at night and clamber up the remote stretch of sandy beach at Galibi. Here, they dig holes and lay their eggs in nests under the sand. Some species, such as the green turtle and the leatherback, are very rare. The turtles are threatened by people who steal their eggs, and they can drown after becoming entangled in fishing nets. Conservationists and indigenous people are working together to protect the turtles in the Galibi nature reserve. To keep track of their numbers, each turtle is measured and tagged when it comes ashore. No fishing is allowed for 9 miles (15 km) off the Galibi coast, and Natives from the local villages work as reserve wardens to watch out for turtle egg thieves. The Native people also earn money from tourists who visit the villages to catch a glimpse of these magnificent creatures.

SOUTH AMERICAN PENGUINS

Along with elephant seals, sea lions, and millions of other birds, the sheer cliffs and barren plains of Peninsula Valdés, in southern Argentina, are the summer homes for more than one million Magellanic penguins. The knee-high males come ashore in early September to prepare a nest in an underground burrow before their mates arrive a few weeks later. After breeding, both parents take turns feeding their chicks until the young are ready to look after themselves. By February, the penguins return to the sea where they remain until the breeding season begins again.

Magellanic penguins are excellent swimmers. Using their wings as paddles, they can speed through the water at up to 15 miles (24 km) an hour.

••••••▶ IN FOCUS: Camel "cousins"

The Andes are home to four relatives of the camel—llama, alpaca, vicuña, and guanaco. Farmers on the altiplano domesticated the llama and alpaca about 4000 B.C., weaving, knitting, and sewing their wool into garments. Today, alpaca wool ends up in the fashion houses of the United States and Europe. Llamas make excellent pack animals. Sure-footed on mountain slopes, they can carry up to 132 pounds (60 kg). Packs of wild vicuña graze on the marshlands of the altiplano. People say that vicuña wool is the softest thing in the world. Guanacos are the larger, southern relatives, with thicker coats to survive the freezing winters in Patagonia.

Guanacos in the Torres del Paine National Park, Chile.

9. THE FUTURE OF SOUTH AMERICA

*A*S MORE PEOPLE ALL OVER THE WORLD MOVE TO CITIES, NEW and less environmentally harmful ways of living together in large numbers need to be found. Curitiba, Brazil, may be a model for the future. Here, local people are involved in planning so that new developments meet their needs. With seventeen parks and 93 miles (150 km) of bicycle lanes, many residents of Curitiba think they live in the world's best city. Nearly two thousand buses carry passengers in special bus lanes that crisscross the city.

Curitiba's transportation network places more importance on public transportation than on automobiles. The network also links different kinds of public transportation, enabling more Curitiba residents to easily and cheaply travel across the city.

Curitiba has ten times as many people as it did fifty years ago, but offers residents, including the city's street children, a chance for a better quality of life. Although not an ideal or complete solution, offices and shops pay street children to do odd jobs to give them a way of supporting themselves.

YOUNG PEACEMAKERS

Colombians are hoping for a more peaceful future. Armed conflict between guerrilla groups and the Colombian army has dragged on for nearly forty years. The guerrillas want the government to give Colombia's poor a better deal, including a fairer share of the

country's land. Some people, however, consider the guerrillas terrorists who use violence and kidnapping to scare people. Today, younger people are speaking out against the war, and older generations are starting to listen. The Children's Movement for Peace is campaigning for the right to a peaceful future, with about one-third of Columbia's young people involved.

A young girl working with UNICEF (the United Nations Children's Fund) and the Children's Peace Movement talks to a soldier about their campaign for peace, in Medellín, Colombia.

DEVELOPMENT THAT LASTS

Important and difficult choices lie ahead for people who live in the Amazon basin. The Amazon rain forest is an immense resource that must be carefully used, and the livelihood of millions depends on it. Brazil plans to create more farms, roads, dams, and natural gas pipelines through the region, but these developments could destroy one-quarter of Brazil's tropical rain forest. There are ways, however, to make money from the forest without destroying it. Small projects that harvest forest products, such as rubber and nuts, already help people in ways that last. Medicines have also been developed from Amazonian plants, such as penicillin, developed from a rain forest fungus, and quinine, a treatment for malaria. These discoveries have already helped people worldwide. As long as the rain forest is kept intact, some scientists hope that a cure for HIV/AIDS may one day be found in a rain forest plant.

STATISTICAL COMPENDIUM

Nation	Area (sq miles)	Population (2003)	Urbanization (% population) 2003	Life expectancy at birth 2002 (in years)	GDP per capita (US$) 2002	Percentage of population under 15 years 2003	Percentage of population over 65 years 2003
Argentina	1,073,116	38,428,000	90.1	74.1	10,880	27	10
Bolivia	424,052	8,808,000	63.4	63.7	2,460	38	4
Brazil	3,299,298	178,470,000	83.1	68.0	7,770	27	5
Chile	292,058	15,805,000	87.0	76.0	9,820	27	7
Colombia	440,645	44,222,000	76.5	72.1	6,370	31	5
Ecuador	105,009	13,003,000	61.8	70.7	3,580	33	5
French Guiana (France)	33,391	178,000	75.4	N/A	N/A	N/A	N/A
Guyana	83,022	765,000	37.6	63.2	4,260	30	5
Paraguay	157,006	5,878,000	57.2	70.7	4,610	39	4
Peru	496,093	27,167,000	73.9	69.7	5,010	32	5
Suriname	63,235	436,000	76.1	71.0	6,590	29	5
Uruguay	68,019	3,415,000	92.6	75.2	7,830	24	13
Venezuela	352,051	25,699,000	87.7	73.6	5,830	32	5

Sources: UN Agencies, World Bank, and Britannica

GLOSSARY

altitude the height of an area of land above sea level, sometimes known as elevation

cartel a group of people, companies, or countries that work together to control the supply and price of a product, e.g. drugs

coca a plant that grows in bushes and is the raw material for producing cocaine

cooperative a company or organization that is jointly owned and run by the people who work there or share in its benefits

coral reef underwater formations made of sea animals with stony skeletons joined together by the thousands

coup a sudden and swift act, such as when a group of people join together to try to overthrow those in power

crossbreeding breeding an animal or plant with a different kind of animal or plant

crust the outer layer of Earth

dictatorship a form of government in which the ruler, or dictator, has complete power

domesticated adapted to suit the needs of people, usually referring to a plant or animal

drug cartel a group of people who work together to control trade in illegal drugs

epiphyte a plant that receives nutrients and moisture from the air and rain and usually grows on the branches of another plant

equator the imaginary line around the center of Earth that divides the northern hemisphere and the southern hemisphere

Fair Trade a system under which producers are paid a fair price for their produce

glacier a huge mass of ice slowly flowing over the land, formed from compressed snow

global warming the gradual warming of Earth's atmosphere as a result of carbon dioxide emissions and other greenhouse gases trapping heat

gourd a bowl made of wood, silver, or a hollowed-out pumpkin

guerrilla a member of an independent and armed group that fights against the rulers of a territory to force a change in the balance of power

hydroelectric power a type of energy generated by fast-flowing water moving through turbine engines

independence the quality or state of having self-governance rather than being under the control of others

indigenous having originated in and living, growing, being produced, or occurring naturally in a particular area or environment

infant mortality the number of babies, out of every one thousand born, who die before the age of one

irrigation the artificial watering of land to help crops grow

landlocked without a coast and surrounded by land

latitude the distance north or south of the equator. The equator is 0 degrees latitude.

Lent the forty days before the religious holiday of Easter when some Christians fast, pray, and give money to the poor

lithium a soft, silver-white substance that is the lightest known metal

malaria a tropical disease transmitted to people by mosquito bites. It causes severe flu-like symptoms and, if not treated, can lead to death in some cases

malnutrition deficiency in the nutrients that are essential for the development and maintenance of the body

multinational company a company that owns and operates manufacturing or service businesses in several countries

nitrate a chemical fertilizer

plantation a type of large farm found in warm or tropical areas

plate a large section of Earth's crust

plateau a flat, raised area of land

Richter scale a scale measuring the amount of energy released by an earthquake

smelting separating metal from rock by melting it in extreme heat in a furnace

subsidy money provided, sometimes by the government, to keep the price of a product or service low or to help pay the producers of a product or service

trade winds tropical winds that blow toward the equator from the northeast (in the northern hemisphere) and the southeast (in the southern hemisphere)

tributary a river or stream that flows into another, normally larger, one

tsunami a very large ocean wave caused by an earthquake or volcanic eruption beneath the sea

urban sprawl the gradual spread of a city center outward

FURTHER INFORMATION

BOOKS TO READ:

Castner, James L. *Surviving in the Rain Forest.* Deep in the Amazon (series). New York: Benchmark Books, 2002.

Hernandez, Roger E. *South America: Facts and Figures.* Discovering South America (series). Philadelphia: Mason Crest Publishers, 2003.

Johnson, Darv. *The Amazon Rain Forest.* Endangered Animals and Habitats (series). San Diego: Lucent Books, 1999.

Morrison, Marion. *Rio de Janeiro.* Great Cities of the World (series). Milwaukee: World Almanac Library, 2004.

Schaffer, David. *Discovering South America's Land, People, and Wildlife: A Myreportlinks.COM Book.* Continents of the World (series). Berkeley Heights, NJ: Enslow Publishers, Inc., 2004.

Sharp, Anne Wallace. *Amazon.* San Diego: Lucent Books, 2003.

Worth, Richard. *Pizarro and the Conquest of the Incan Empire in World History.* In World History (series). Berkeley Heights, NJ: Enslow Publishers, Inc., 2000.

USEFUL WEB SITES:

kids.ran.org/kidscorner/index.html
Rainforest Action Network's Web site for young people.

www.infoplease.com/atlas/southamerica.html
Interactive atlas gives detailed information about the countries of South America.

www.mnsu.edu/emuseum/prehistory/latinamerica/south/sites/machu_picchu.html
View photographs of Machu Picchu and learn more about the history of this ancient place.

www.mrdowling.com/712southamerica.html
Interesting facts about the land and people of South America.

www.odci.gov/cia/publications/factbook/
The CIA World Facts Web site, giving facts and figures on every country.

www.pbs.org/journeyintoamazonia/
PBS' site on life in the Amazon basin.

www.survival-international.org/world.htm
Survival International's site provides current information on the tribal people of South America and the challenges they face.

www.worldwildlife.org/wildplaces/amazon/index.cfm
Learn more about the Amazon rain forest and efforts to protect it.

INDEX

ABOUT THE AUTHOR

Simon Scoones is Education Project Manager for Worldaware, where he is the author of globaleye.org.uk Web site for schools, as well as other printed resources about global issues. He is also a teacher-training tutor at the Institute of Education, University of London. He has taught Geography and Social Studies in the United Kingdom and in international schools in Singapore and Antwerp, Belgium. He has written a number of books on environment and development issues for young people, and he has traveled across six continents.